LIFE AS I SEE IT

LIFE STORIES

SREELAKSHMI N NAIR

Copyright © Sreelakshmi N Nair
All Rights Reserved.

To,

My beloved son Shantanu without whom I would have never got this second life.

My Mom, Dad, Sister, Husband and all those who hold a special place in my heart.

Contents

Acknowledgements

I cannot express enough thanks to my dear husband who helped me make this book a reality.

My Mom, who taught me to chase my dreams and to that best friend who lifts me up whenever I fall down.

1. An Ode to Chai!

When the sun peeps in through the wooden windows
And sparkles its shine upon the green meadows,
All I long for is a piping hot cup of Chai
its white heavenly vapors rising high.
The room gets filled with its divine scent
Of cardamom, cinnamon and other strongly brewed
contents.
The brewing Chai I can no longer resist
With a racing heart I rush for our tryst.
My heart attains supreme bliss,
As I slowly lift the glass for my morning kiss.
And as it melts in my mouth,
It quenches all my thirst from the last night's drouth.
Oh Chai, thanks for existing
Thanks for being that magical potion that I gulp down
unresisting.

2. Footprints in the lonely world

She wandered like a dream,
On the calm, breezy beach.
Her tiny brown eyes
Captivated my weary spirit…
Her face told an unspoken story,
As dark as the starless sky.
She was a young sapling,
Hiding from light of the world.
She was a tiny sinless soul,
But features, as sharp as the flaming sword.
A lifetime of agony she enshrouded in her face,
But jumped around like an insouciant butterfly.
Her unswept feet and unkempt hair,
As charming as the saints in heaven.
She locked me with her looks as deep as the ocean beside her,
I braced myself and enquired;
"Oh my cute little lonely soul, why do you wander in
solitude"?
She smiled, a smile that stabbed ahundred knives into my
heart.
A packet of peanuts she offered me with love and walked
away into solitude.

I let her float in her solitary world.

My questions left unanswered…..

3. My Magician

Yesterday he was a stranger
A magician, that took me
to places dark and exotic;
showed me what life was like
in places untraveled and mystic!
The magic in his eyes,
made my pupils dilate.
The magic in his smile,
made my mind elate.
The magic in his voice,
healed my deep wear.
The magic in his touch,
ignited my inner flare.
With his hypnotic wand he put me to sleep.
And then I woke up,
I woke up from my dreamy sleep.
There he was,
No more a stranger; he was all mine!
His gentle hands caressed my hair,
took away my agony and pain.
I closed my eyes,
etched that moment in my heart.
The clock stopped ticking; the sun stopped setting.

For here I was, a tranquil sea shore,
longing to melt and blend into my giant magical wave!

4. Rainy Days

The sky blushed and blushed;
As its face the red overcast painted and brushed.
The golden leaves from the mighty trees
Fell down swaying on the lonely streets.
The smell of the virgin mud lingered in the air,
As the first drop of rain descended like a prayer.
The birds flew in harmony,
Rushing to their nests like a symphony.
And when it began pouring,
The whispering breeze switched to a wild wind roaring!
The swaying leaves began swirling in the air,
As meddled up like the medusa's hair.
While the overcast changed from red to black,
The sky longed to get its blush back.
And then the season began……
The season of rains, storm, lightning and thunder,
The season of wild intense love and threatening sunder!

5. The Secret

My sweet little secret
Safe as a child on its mother's breast.
Neither light nor plight steps in
But only my heart's lullaby seeps in.
Inside my shell lies the secret pearl,
Separate me from it, and I am no more.
I close my eyes, I see you,
I count my breath, I hear you.
I carry you wherever I go,
For it hurts and bleeds when I let you go.
Day and night,
you are my guiding light.
Even death can't make us part,
For even in grave, you will be close to my heart.

6. The Summer Vaccation

Those 20 days were like heaven;
Every 90's kid's obsession;
Yes, the long awaited summer vacation.
Meant for cousin's assimilation.
The blazing sun and the scorching heat,
Never knocked down our spirit!
Mango orchards and coconut farms;
the perfect playgrounds for us bee swarms.
Flavored lassis and tender coconut water,
quenched our thirst in the weather that got hotter.
And at sun set, we returned with mud and dirt,
and other precious stones of the outskirts.
When we flocked back to our nests at dusk,
To greet us there was filter coffee and jasmine musk!
Gone are those days filled with laughter and fun,
Days of sweat and the mighty sun!